a little brown notebook

Scenes from
Jane Eyre
by Charlotte Brontë

Illustrated by Sandra Russell

M·Q·P

Dreadful to me was the coming home in the raw twilight, with nipped fingers and toes, and a heart saddened by the chidings of Bessie, the nurse, and humbled by the consciousness of my physical inferiority to Eliza, John and Georgiana Reed.

'You are a dependant mamma says; you have no money; your father left you none; you ought to beg; and not to live here with gentlemen's children like us, and eat the same meals we do, and wear clothes at our mamma's expense.'

When I saw him lift and poise the book and stand in act to hurl it, I instinctively started aside with a cry of alarm: not soon enough, however; the volume was flung, it hit me, and I fell, striking my head against the door and cutting it.

'Take her away to the red-room, and lock her in there.'

All John Reed's violent tyrannies, all his sisters' proud indifference, all his mother's aversion, all the servant's partiality, turned up in my disturbed mind like a dark deposit in a turbid well. Why was I always suffering, always browbeaten, always accused, forever condemned?

Why could I never please? Why was it useless to try to win any one's favour?

'I should wish her to be brought up in a manner suiting her prospects,' continued my benefactress; 'to be made useful, to be kept humble.'

'Lowood: plain fare, simple attire, unsophisticated accommodations, hardy and active habits: such is the order of the day in the house and its inhabitants.'

'I am glad you are no relation of mine. I will never call you aunt again as long as I live. I will never come to see you when I am grown up; and if anyone asks me how I liked you, and how you treated me I will say the very thought of you makes me sick, and that you treated me with miserable cruelty.'

'How dare you affirm that, Jane Eyre?'

'How dare I, Mrs Reed? How dare I? Because it is the truth ... People think you are a good woman, but you are bad, hard-hearted. You are deceitful!'

I passed from compartment to compartment, from passage to passage, of a large and irregular building; till emerging from the total and somewhat dreary silence pervading that portion of the house we had traversed, we came upon the hum of many voices ... a congregation of girls of every age, from nine or ten to twenty.

A great tumult succeeded for some minutes, during which Miss Miller repeatedly exclaimed, 'Silence!' and 'Order!' When it subsided, I saw them all drawn up in four semicircles, before four chairs, placed at the four tables: all held books in their hands, and a great book, like a Bible, lay on each table, before the vacant seat. A pause of some seconds succeeded, filled up by the low, vague, hum of numbers: Miss Miller walked from class to class, hushing this indefinite sound.

Miss Miller assumed the fourth vacant chair, which was that nearest the door, and around which the smallest of the children were assembled: to this inferior class I was called, and placed at the bottom of it.

The refectory was a great, low-ceiled, gloomy room; on two long tables soaked basins of something hot, which, however, to my dismay, sent forth an odour far from inviting. I saw a universal manifestation of discontent when the fumes of the repast met the nostrils of those destined to swallow it; from the van of the procession, the tall girls of the first class, rose the whispered words –

'Disgusting! The porridge is burnt again!'

My first quarter at Lowood seemed an age, and not the golden age either; it comprised an irksome struggle with difficulties in habituating myself to new rules and unwonted tasks. The fear of failure in these points harassed me worse than the physical hardships of my lot, though these were no trifles.

'Madam ... Should any little accidental disappointment of the appetite occur, such as the spoiling of a meal, the under or the over-dressing of a dish, the incident ought not to be neutralised by replacing with something more delicate the comfort lost, thus pampering the body and obviating the aim of this institution; it ought to be improved to the spiritual edification of the pupils, by encouraging them to evince fortitude under the temporary privation ... Oh, madam, when you put bread and cheese, instead of burnt porridge, into these children's mouths, you may indeed feed their vile bodies, but you little think how you starve their immortal souls!'

'My dear children,' pursued the black marble clergyman with pathos, 'this is a sad, a melancholy occasion; for it becomes my duty to warn you that this girl, who might be one of God's own lambs, is a little castaway – not a member of the true flock, but evidently an interloper and an alien. You must be on your guard against her; you must shun her example – if necessary, avoid her company, exclude her from your sports, and shut her out from your converse. Teachers, you must watch her; keep your eyes on her movements, weigh well her words, scrutinise her actions, punish her body to save her soul ... this girl is – a liar!'

Some one approached: I started up – again Helen Burns was near me; the fading fires just showed her coming up the long, vacant room; she brought my coffee and bread ...

'Helen, why do you stay with a girl whom everybody believes to be a liar?' ...

'If all the world hated you, and believed you wicked, while your own conscience approved you, and absolved you from guilt, you would not be without friends.'

'Well, now, Jane, you know, or at least I will tell you, that when a criminal is accused, he is always allowed to speak in his own defence. You have been charged with falsehood; defend yourself to me as well as you can.'

That forest dell, where Lowood lay, was the cradle of fog and fog bred pestilence; which, quickening with the quickening spring, crept into the Orphan Asylum, breathed typhus through its crowded schoolroom and dormitory, and, ere May arrived, transformed the seminary into a hospital.

Semi-starvation and neglected colds had predisposed most of the pupils to receive infection: forty-five out of the eighty girls lay ill at one time.

'I came to see you, Helen: I heard you were very ill, and I could not sleep till I had spoken to you.'

'You came to bid me good-bye, then: you are just in time probably.'

'Are you going somewhere, Helen? Are you going home?'

'Yes; to my long home – my last home.'

'No, no, Helen!' I stopped distressed. While I tried to devour my tears, a fit of coughing seized Helen; it did not, however wake the nurse ... Miss Temple, on returning to her own room at dawn, had found me laid in a little crib; my face against Helen Burn's shoulder, my arms round her neck. I was asleep, and Helen was – dead.

My world had for some years been in Lowood; my experience had been of its rules and systems; now I remembered that the real world was wide ... I had had no communication by letter, or message with the outer world. School rules, school duties, school habits and notions, and voices, and faces, and phrases, and costumes, and preferences, and antipathies: such was what I knew of existence. And now I felt that it was not enough. I tired of the routine of eight years in one afternoon. I desired liberty.

A phase of my life was closing to-night, a new one opening to-morrow: impossible to slumber in the interval; I must watch feverishly while the change was being accomplished.

A snug, small room; a round table by a cheerful fire; an arm-chair, high-backed and old-fashioned, wherein sat the neatest imaginable little elderly lady, in widow's cap, black silk gown, and snowy muslin apron ... She was occupied in knitting; a large cat sat demurely at her feet; nothing, in short, was wanting to complete the beau-ideal of domestic comfort. A more reassuring introduction for a new governess could scarcely be conceived: there was no grandeur to overwhelm, no stateliness to embarrass.

Externals have a great effect on the young. I thought that a fairer era of life was beginning for me, one that was to have its flowers and pleasures, as well as its thorns and toils.

'Is Mr Rochester an exacting, fastidious sort of man?'...

'He is rather peculiar, perhaps ... it is not easy to describe – nothing striking, but you feel it when he speaks to you: you cannot be always sure whether he is in jest or earnest, whether he is pleased or the contrary: you don't thoroughly understand him.'

While I paced softly on, the last sound I expected to hear in so still a region, a laugh, struck my ears. It was a curious laugh – distinct, formal, mirthless. I stopped ... the laugh was as tragic, as preternatural a laugh as any I ever heard; and, but that it was high noon, and that no circumstance of ghostliness accompanied the curious cachinnation; but that neither scene nor season favoured fear, I should have been superstitiously afraid.

Something of daylight still lingered, and the moon was waxing bright; I could see him plainly. His figure was enveloped in a riding cloak, fur collared and steel clasped; its details were not apparent, but I traced the general points of middle height, and considerable breadth of chest. He had a dark face, with stern features and a heavy brow; his eyes and gathered eyebrows looked ireful and thwarted just now; he was past youth, but had not reached middle age; perhaps he might be thirty-five. I felt no fear of him, and but little shyness. Had he been a handsome, heroic-looking young gentleman, I should not have dared to stand thus questioning him against his will.

'When I was as old as you, I was a feeling fellow enough; partial to the unfledged, unfostered, and unlucky; but fortune has knocked me about since … and now I flatter myself I am hard and tough … Nature meant me to be, on the whole, a good man, Miss Eyre; one of the better kind, and you see I am not so.'

His deportment had now for some weeks been more uniform towards me than at first ... when summoned by formal invitation to his presence, I was honoured by a cordiality of reception that made me feel I really possessed the power to amuse him ... I heard him talk with relish. It was his nature to be communicative ... I felt at times as if he were my relation rather than my master: yet he was imperious sometimes still ... so gratified did I become with this new interest added to life, that I ceased to pine after kindred.

He was proud, sardonic, harsh to inferiority of every description: in my secret soul I knew that his great kindness to me was balanced by unjust severity to many others.

A dream had scarcely approached my ear, when it fled affrighted, scared by a marrow-freezing incident enough.

This was a demonic laugh – low, suppressed, and deep – uttered, as it seemed, at the very keyhole of my chamber door ... the unnatural sound was reiterated. My first impulse was to rise and fasten the bolt; my next again to cry out ... while looking to the right hand and left; I became further aware of a strong smell of burning.

Something creaked: it was a door ajar; and that door was Mr Rochester's, and the smoke rushed in a cloud from thence ... in an instant, I was within the chamber. Tongues of flame darted round the bed: the curtains were on fire. In the midst of blaze and vapour, Mr Rochester lay stretched motionless, in deep sleep.

'Wake! wake!' I cried. I shook him, but he only murmured and turned ... Not a moment could be lost; the very sheets were kindling. I rushed to the basin and ewer; fortunately, one was wide and the other deep, and both were filled with water. I heaved them up, deluged the bed and its occupant.

'I knew ... you would do me good in some
way, at some time: I saw it in your eyes when I
first beheld you: their expression and smile
did not ... strike delight to my very inmost heart
so for nothing.'

'You,' I said 'a favourite with Mr Rochester? You gifted with the power of pleasing him? You of importance to him in any way? ... How dared you? Poor stupid dupe! ... It does good to no woman to be flattered by her superior, who cannot possible intend to marry her; and it is madness in all women to let a secret love kindle within them.

'Listen, then, Jane Eyre, to your sentence: to-morrow, place the glass before you, and draw in chalk your picture ... write under it, "Portrait of a Governess, dis-connected, poor, and plain".'

And did I now think Miss Ingram such a choice as Mr Rochester would be likely to make? I could not tell – I did not know his taste in female beauty. If he liked the majestic, she was the very type of majesty; then she was accomplished, sprightly. Most gentlemen would admire her, I thought; and that he did admire her, I already seemed to have obtained proof: to remove the last shade of doubt, it remained but to see them together.

I have told you, reader, that I had learnt to love Mr Rochester: I could not unlove him now, merely because I found that he had ceased to notice me – because I might pass hours in his presence and he would never once turn his eyes in my direction – because I saw all his attentions appropriated by a great lady, who scorned to touch me with the hem of her robes as she passed ... Miss Ingram was a mark beneath my jealousy: she was too inferior to excite the feeling. Pardon the seeming paradox; I mean what I say. She was very showy, but she was not genuine; she had a fine person, many brilliant attainments, but her mind was poor, her heart barren.

'Are you aware, Mr Rochester, that a stranger has arrived here since you left this morning?'

'A stranger! – no; who can it be? I expected no one; is he gone?'

'No; he said he had known you long, and that he could take the liberty of installing himself here till you returned.'

'The devil he did! Did he give his name?'

'His name is Mason, sir; and he comes from the West Indies; from Spanish town, in Jamaica, I think.'

... At a late hour, after I had been in bed some time, I heard the visitors repair to their chambers; I distinguished Mr Rochester's voice, and heard him say, 'This way, Mason; this is your room.'

My pulse stopped: my heart stood still; my stretched arm was paralysed. The cry died, and was not renewed. Indeed, whatever being uttered that fearful shriek could not soon repeat it: not the wildest-winged condor on the Andes could, twice in succession, send out such a yell from the cloud shrouding his eyrie. The thing delivering such utterance must rest ere it could repeat the effort.

It came out of the third story; for it passed overhead. And overhead ... yes, in the room just above my chamber-ceiling ... I now heard a struggle: a deadly one it seemed from the noise; and a half-smothered voice shouted.

I began and dressed myself carefully. The sounds I had heard after the scream, and the words that had been uttered, had probably been heard only by me; for they had proceeded from the room above mine: but they assured me that it was not a servant's dream which had thus struck horror through the house; and that the explanation Mr Rochester had given was merely an invention framed to pacify his guests. I dressed, then, to be ready for emergencies ...

'Am I wanted?' I asked.

'Are you up?' asked the voice I expected to hear, namely, my master's.

'Here, Jane!' he said; and I walked round to the other side of the large bed, which with its drawn curtains concealed a considerable portion of the chamber. An easy-chair was near the bed-head: a man sat in it, dressed with the exception of his coat; he was still; his head leant back; his eyes were closed. Mr Rochester held the candle over him; I recognized in his pale and seemingly lifeless face – the stranger, Mason: I saw, too, that his linen on one side, and one arm, was almost soaked in blood ...

And this man I bent over – this commonplace, quiet stranger – how had he become involved in the web of horror? and why had the fury flown at him?

I was summoned downstairs by a message that some one wanted me in Mrs Fairfax's room. On repairing thither, I found a man waiting for me, having the appearance of a gentleman's servant ...

'Mrs Reed ... a stroke. She was three days without speaking: but last Tuesday she seemed rather better: she appeared as if she wanted to say something, and kept making signs to my wife and mumbling ... she was pronouncing your name; and at last she made out of the words, "Bring Jane – fetch Jane Eyre: I want to speak to her" ... I should like to take you back with me early to-morrow morning.'

I reached the lodge at Gateshead about five o'clock in the afternoon ... 'I trust I am not too late. How is Mrs Reed? – Alive still, I hope.'

It is a happy thing that time quells the longings of vengeance and hushes the promptings of rage and aversion. I had left this woman in bitterness and hate, and I came back to her now ... I had once vowed that I would never call her aunt again: I thought it no sin to forget and break that vow now.

'Read the letter,' she said …
Madam, will you have the goodness to send me
the address of my niece, Jane Eyre, and to tell
me how she is … I wish to adopt her during my
life, and bequeath her at my death whatever I
may have to leave …
  It was dated three years back.

'Must I move on sir?' I asked. 'Must I leave Thornfield?'

'I believe you must, Jane. I am sorry, Janet.'

'In about a month I hope to be a bridegroom ... I shall myself look out for employment and an asylum for you.'

'I have ... heard of a place that I think will suit ... Ireland.'

'It is a long way off sir.'

'From what, Jane?'

'From England and from Thornfield.'

'I grieve to leave Thornfield: I love Thornfield: I love it, because I have lived in it a full and delightful life – momentarily at least. I have not been trampled on. I have not been petrified. I have not been buried with inferior minds, and excluded from every glimpse of communion with what is bright and energetic and high. I have talked, face to face, with what I reverence, with what I delight in – with an original, a vigorous, an expanded mind. I have known you, Mr Rochester; and it strikes me with terror and anguish to feel I absolutely must be torn from you for ever. I see the necessity of departure; and it is like looking on the necessity of death.'

'But Jane, I summon you as my wife: it is you only I intend to marry.'

'I would not – I could not – marry Miss Ingram. You – you strange, you almost unearthly thing! – I love you as my own flesh.'

Before I left my bed in the morning, little Adele came running in to tell me that the great horse-chestnut at the bottom of the orchard had been struck by lightning in the night, and half of it split away.

'I am sorry to grieve you,' pursued Mrs Fairfax; 'but you are so young, and so little acquainted with men, I wished to put you on your guard. It is an old saying that "all is not gold that glitters"; and in this case I do fear there will be something found to be different to what either you or I expect.'

'I hope all will be right in the end,' she said: 'but, believe me, you cannot be too careful. Try and keep Mr Rochester at a distance: distrust yourself as well as him. Gentlemen in his station are not accustomed to marry their governesses.'

The new life was to commence to-morrow.

I continued in dreams the idea of a dark and gusty night .... I experienced a strange, regretful consciousness of some barrier dividing us.

'I dreamt another dream, sir: that Thornfield Hall was a dreary ruin, the retreat of bats and owls. I thought that of all the stately front nothing remained but a shell-like wall.'

There was a light on the dressing-table, and the door of the closet, where, before going to bed, I had hung my wedding-dress and veil, stood open.

The shape standing before me had never crossed my eyes within the precincts of Thornfield Hall before; the height, the contour were new to me.

'Sir, it removed my veil from its gaunt head, rent it in two parts, and flinging both on the floor, trampled on them.'

Just at my bedside the figure stopped: the fiery eyes glared upon me.

'But, sir, when I said to myself on rising this morning, and when I looked round the room to gather courage and comfort from the cheerful aspect of each familiar object in full daylight, there – on the carpet – I saw what gave the distinct lie to my hypothesis – the veil, torn from top to bottom in two halves!'

'Wilt thou have this woman for thy wedded wife?' – when a distinct and near voice said – 'The marriage cannot go on: I declare the existence of an impediment.'

'Mr Rochester has a wife now living.'

'Bigamy is an ugly word! – I meant, however, to be a bigamist; but fate has out-manoeuvred me.'

'Bertha Mason is mad; and she came of a mad family; idiots and maniacs through three generations!'

Whether beast or human being, one could not, at first sight tell: it grovelled, seemingly, on all fours; it snatched and growled like some strange wild animal.

I was in my own room as usual – just myself, without obvious change: nothing had smitten me, or scathed me, or maimed me. And yet where was the Jane Eyre of yesterday? – where was her life? – where were her prospects?

My hopes were all dead.

'But that I must leave him decidedly, instantly, entirely, is intolerable. I cannot do it.'

But then a voice within me averred that I could do it ...

I cleared and steadied my voice to reply: 'All is changed about me, sir; I must change, too – there is no doubt of that; and to avoid fluctuations of feeling, and continual combats with recollections and associations, there is only one way – Adele must have a new governess, sir.'

I must begin a new existence among strange faces
and strange scenes.

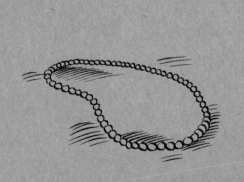

'It cannot be too early to commence the task I have to fulfil,' thought I. I rose: I was dressed. I knew where to find in my drawers some linen, a locket, a ring. In seeking these articles, I encountered the beads of a pearl necklace Mr Rochester had forced me to accept a few days ago. I left that; it was not mine: it was the visionary bride's who had melted in air.

While I sat I heard wheels, and saw a coach come on. I stood up and lifted my hand; it stopped ... I asked for what sum he would take me there; he said thirty shillings; I answered I had but twenty; well, he would try to make it do.

The coachman has set me down at a place called Whitcross.

I discover that I forgot to take my parcel out of the pocket of the coach, where I had placed it for safety; there it remains, there it must remain; and now, I am absolutely destitute.

Not a tie holds me to human society at this moment ... I have no relative but the universal mother, Nature: I will seek her breast and ask repose.

What was I to do? Where to go?

I had a small silk handkerchief tied round my throat; I had my gloves. I could hardly tell how men and women in extremities of destitution proceeded. I did not know whether either of these articles would be accepted: probably they would not; but I must try.

Much exhausted, and suffering greatly now for want of food, I turned aside into a lane and sat down under the hedge ... A pretty little house stood at the top of the lane, with a garden before it, exquisitely neat and brilliantly blooming ... What business had I to approach the white door or touch the glittering knocker?

I believe I should have begged a piece of bread;
for I was now brought low.

While the rain descends so, must I lay my head on the cold, drenched ground? I fear I cannot do otherwise: for who will receive me? But it will be very dreadful, with this feeling of hunger, faintness, chill, and the sense of desolation – this total prostration of hope. In all likelihood, though, I should die before morning.

I discriminated the rough stones of a low wall ...
a whitish object gleamed before me; it was a gate
– a wicket; it moved on its hinges as I touched it
... the silhouette of a house rose to view.

A group of more interest appeared near the hearth, sitting still amidst the rosy peace and warmth suffusing it. Two young graceful women ... sat, one in a low rocking-chair, the other on a lower stool ... I had nowhere seen such faces as theirs: and yet, as I gazed on them, I seemed intimate with every lineament.

As I groped out the door, and knocked at it hesitatingly ... Hannah opened.

'What do you want?' she inquired in a voice of surprise, as she surveyed me by the light of the candle she held ...'What is your business here at this hour?'

'I want a night's shelter in an outhouse or anywhere, and a morsel of bread to eat.'

'I can but die,' I said, 'and I believe in God. Let me try to wait His will in silence.'

'All men must die,' said a voice quite close at hand; 'but all are not condemned to meet a lingering and premature doom, such as yours would be if you perished here of want ... Young woman, rise, and pass before me into the house.'

My clothes hung loose on me, for I was much wasted; but I covered deficiencies with a shawl, and once more, clean and respectable-looking.

Mr St John ... was easy enough to examine. Had he been a statue instead of a man, he could not have been easier ... he seemed of a reserved, an abstracted, and even of a brooding nature.

'I believe you will accept the post I offer you,' said he, 'and hold it for a while ... I mean now to open a second school for girls. I have hired a building for the purpose, with a cottage of two rooms attached to it for the mistress's house. Her salary will be thirty pounds a year: her house is already furnished, very simply, but sufficiently ... Will you be this mistress?'

It was sheltered, and I wanted a safe asylum; it was plodding – but then, compared with that of a governess in a rich house, it was independent.

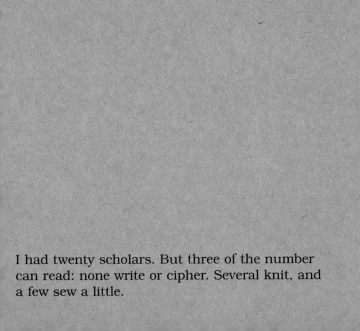

I had twenty scholars. But three of the number
can read: none write or cipher. Several knit, and
a few sew a little.

After a day passed in honourable exertion
amongst my scholars, an evening spent in
drawing or reading contentedly alone ...

What he suddenly saw on this blank paper, it was impossible for me to tell; but something had caught his eye. He took it up with a snatch; he looked at the edge; then shot a glance at me, inexpressibly peculiar and quite incomprehensible: a glance that seemed to take and make a note of every point in my shape, face and dress.

'What is the matter?' I asked.

'Nothing in the world,' was the reply; and replacing the paper, I saw him dexterously tear a narrow slip from the margin. It disappeared in his glove; and, with one hasty nod and 'good-afternoon', he vanished.

And the pocket-book was again deliberately produced, opened, sought through; from one of its compartments was extracted a shabby slip of paper, hastily torn off: I recognized in its texture and its stains of ultramarine, and lake, and vermilion, the ravished margin of the portrait cover. Mr Rivers got up, held it close to my eyes: and I read, traced in Indian ink, in my own handwriting, the words 'JANE EYRE.'

'Mr Eyre of Madeira, is dead; that he has left you all his property, and that you are now rich – merely that – nothing more.'

'I! – rich?'

'Yes, you rich – quite an heiress ... You must prove your identity, of course,' resumed St John presently: 'a step which will offer no difficulties.'

'Do let me speak,' I said; 'let me have one moment to draw breath and reflect.' I paused – he stood before me, hat in hand, looking composed enough. I resumed –

'Your mother was my father's sister?'

'Yes.'

'My aunt, consequently?'

He bowed.

'My uncle John was your uncle John? You, Diana, and Mary are his sister's children, as I am his brother's child?'

'Undeniably.'

'You three, then, are my cousins; half our blood on each side flows from the same source?'

'You were serious when I told you you had got a fortune; and now, for a matter of no moment, you are excited.'

'What can you mean? it may be of no moment to you; you have sisters and don't care for a cousin; but I had nobody; and now three relations ... are born into my world full-grown.'

Those who had saved my life, whom, till this hour, I had loved barrenly, I could now benefit.

'What aim, what purpose, what ambition in life
have you now?'

St John was a good man; but I began to feel he had spoken truth of himself when he said he was hard and cold. The humanities of life had no attraction for him – its peaceful enjoyments no charm. Literally, he lived only to aspire.

By degrees, he acquired a certain influence over me that took away my liberty of mind: his praise and notice were more restraining than his indifference. I could no longer talk or laugh freely when he was by, because a tiresomely importunate instinct reminded me that vivacity (at least in me) was distasteful to him ... He wanted to train me to an elevation I could never reach.

The thing was as impossible as to mould my irregular features to his correct and classic pattern, to give to my changeable green eyes the sea-blue tint and solemn lustre of his own.

'Jane, come with me to India: come as my helpmeet and fellow-labourer ... God and nature intended you for a missionary's wife. It is not personal, but mental endowments they have given you: you are formed for labour, not for love. A missionary's wife you must – shall be.'

'I have an answer for you – hear it. I have watched you ever since we first met: I have made you my study for ten months. I have proved you in time by sundry tests: and what have I seen and elicited? In the village school I found you could perform well, punctually, uprightly, labour uncongenial to your habits and inclinations ...'

'I am ready to go to India, if I may go free.'

'Your answer requires a commentary,' he said; 'it is not clear.'

'You have hitherto been my adopted brother – I, your adopted sister: let us continue as such: you and I had better not marry.'

' ... I want a wife: the sole helpmeet I can influence efficiently in life, and retain absolutely till death.'

I shuddered as he spoke: I felt his influence in my marrow – his hold on my limbs.

'You cannot – you ought not. Do you think God will be satisfied with half an oblation? Will He accept a mutilated sacrifice? It is the cause of God I advocate: it is under His standard I enlist you. I cannot accept on His behalf a divided allegiance: it must be entire.'

' ... do not forget that if you reject it, it is not me you deny, but God. Through my means, He opens to you a noble career; as my wife only can you enter upon it.'

'A female curate, who is not my wife, would never suit me. With me, then it seems, you cannot go ...'

My heart beat fast and thick ... I saw nothing,
but I heard a voice somewhere cry –
  'Jane! Jane! Jane!' – nothing more.
  'O God! what is it?' I gasped.

And it was the voice of a human being – a known, loved, well-remembered voice – that of Edward Fairfax Rochester; and it spoke in pain and woe, wildly, eerily, urgently.

'I am coming!' I cried. 'Wait for me! Oh, I will come!' I flew to the door and looked into the passage: it was dark. I ran out into the garden: it was void.

'Where are you?' I exclaimed.

'I will know something of him whose voice seemed last night to summon me. Letters have proved of no avail – personal inquiry shall replace them.'

How fast I walked! How I ran sometimes! How I looked forward to catch the first view of the well-known woods! With what feelings I welcomed single trees I knew and familiar glimpses of meadow and hill between them!

I looked with timorous joy towards a stately
house; I saw a blackened ruin.

' ... No one is living there. I suppose you are a stranger in these parts, or you would have heard what happened last autumn – Thornfield Hall is quite a ruin: it was burnt down just about harvest-time. A dreadful calamity! such an immense quantity of valuable property destroyed ... It was a terrible spectacle: I witnessed it myself.'

' ... he went up to the attics when all was
burning above and below, and got the servants
out of the beds and helped them down himself,
and went back to get his mad wife out of her cell
... she was on the roof, where she was standing,
waving her arms above the battlements, and
shouting out till they could hear her a mile off ...'

9

' ... She was a big woman, and had long black hair: we could see it streaming against the flames ... she yelled and gave a spring, and the next minute she lay smashed on the pavement.'

'He is stone-blind,' he said at last. 'Yes, he is stone-blind, is Mr Edward [Rochester] ... He is now helpless, indeed – blind, and a cripple.'

The darkness of natural as well as of sylvan dusk gathered over me. I looked round in search of another road. There was none: all was interwoven stem, columnar trunk, dense summer foliage – no opening anywhere.

It opened slowly: a figure came out into the twilight and stood on the step – a man without a hat. He stretched forth his hand as if to feel whether it rained. Dusk as it was, I had recognized him; it was my master, Edward Fairfax Rochester, and no other.

I saw a change: that looked desperate and brooding – that reminded me of some wronged and fettered wild beast or bird, dangerous to approach in his sullen woe. The caged eagle, whose gold-ringed eyes cruelty has extinguished, might look as looked that sightless Samson.

'Jane Eyre! – Jane Eyre!' was all he said.

'My dear master,' I answered, 'I am Jane Eyre: I have found you out – I come back to you.'

' ... I will be your neighbour, your nurse, your housekeeper. I find you lonely: I will be your companion – to read to you, to walk with you, to sit with you, to wait on you, to be eyes and hands to you. Cease to look so melancholy, my dear master; you shall not be left desolate, so long as I live.'

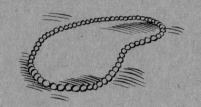

'Cruel, cruel deserter! Oh, Jane, what did I feel when I discovered you had fled from Thornfield, and when I could nowhere find you: and, after examining your apartment, ascertained that you had taken no money, nor anything which could serve as an equivalent!'

'Ah! Jane. But I want a wife.'

'Do you, sir?'

'Yes: it is news to you?'

'Of course: you said nothing about it before.'

'Is it unwelcome news?'

'That depends on circumstances, sir – on your choice.'

'Which you shall make for me, Jane. I will abide by your decision.'

'Choose then, sir – her who loves you best.'

'I will at least choose – her I love best. Jane, will you marry me?'

'Yes, sir.'

'I was in my own room and sitting by the window, which was open … I longed for thee Janet! … the alpha and omega of my heart's wishes broke involuntarily from my lips in the words, – "Jane! Jane! Jane!"' '

'In spirit, I believe, we must have met. You no doubt were, at that hour, in unconscious sleep, Jane: perhaps your soul wandered from its cell to comfort mine; for those were your accents as certain as I live, they were yours!'

Reader, I married him.

One morning at the end of two years, as I was writing a letter to his dictation, he came and bent over me, and said –

'Jane, have you a glittering ornament round your neck?'

I had a gold watch-chain: I answered 'Yes.'

'And have you a pale blue dress on?'

I had ...

He went up to London. He had the advice of an eminent oculist; and he eventually recovered the sight of that one eye ... the sky is no longer a blank to him – the earth no longer a void.

Published by Museum Quilts (UK) Inc.
254-258 Goswell Road, London EC1V 7EB

Copyright © Museum Quilts Publications, Inc. 1997

Illustrations © Sandra Russell 1997

ISBN: 1 897954 82 4

Printed and bound in Hong Kong